But GOD...

A Spiritual Journey
Illuminating the
Power of Forgiveness

A Memoir by Gloria Perry-Stevens

GLORIA PERRY-STEVENS

But GOD…

ISBN:9781687569141 (KDP AMAZON)
ISBN:9781078713320 (BARNES AND NOBLES PAPERBACK)
ISBN:9781078711937 (BARNES AND NOBLES HARDBACK)
Library of Congress Number: 2019912708

DEDICATION

This book is dedicated to all those who have found themselves paralyzed by unforgiveness with what seems to be no other way. Let this book be a vehicle for sharing the importance in order to heal, this has to be a necessary act. Let go of any attachments to the act itself, move on; forgive the sinner, but not the sin. Don't live your life in bondage.

With harm and pain so inherent to the human condition, forgiveness is a powerful countermeasure. My prayer is that you connect yourself to the one that showed the ultimate forgiveness. Our Lord and Savior Jesus Christ. It's never too late.

God Bless!

GLORIA PERRY-STEVENS

CONTENTS

GLORIA PERRY-STEVENS

ACKNOWLEDGMENTS

A special thanks to my friends and family and to all those who listened and encouraged me to write this book. You will never be forgotten. I would love to name you all but there are so many, and I wouldn't want to forget anyone, you already know who you are.

A very special thanks to a wonderful caring and compassionate "Woman of God" who took time out of her busy schedule to hear with her ears but listened with her heart as she captured me in this story and felt the necessity I felt in trying to help me complete this journey. I love you dearly, Candace Richardson.

My brothers and sisters may the blessings of God sustain you! God loves you and so do I. Just don't only see me as the woman, but the little girl that became THIS woman. The one that looked for love in all the wrong places.

"But God," I Thank you that the darkness didn't hide me from you.

INTRODUCTION

This is a story of truth and it is important for me to reveal the crucial events that caused or contributed to my life story. Yet, I still have joy. My purpose for writing my story is to show the life and face of "forgiveness" by God's invisible hand navigating me through a time when I really didn't know him.

It's about a God who kept me from being a murderer, a God who kept me from committing suicide, a God who kept me silent, and a God who set me free. I have been compelled to share my life story. A true testament of God's grace and my determination to survive after a life of molestation, parental mistreatment, beatings, gang rape, and kidnapping.

Like others, we have shameful acts in our past and the memories that accompany them. Those hurtful recollections that taunt us in the middle of the night.

There's so much we wish we could undo or redo. But, thank God for the grace that not only forgives sin but also uses it to make us better than before.

Please know this one thing, that God is not a respecter of persons as what man is. He doesn't care about your status or popularity. What He did for me, He can do for you. Come, it's time to get set free. As I always say, "I've been through the fire, but I don't smell like the smoke."

"But God!"

SCRIPTURE I LIVE BY

"Father forgive them for they know not what they do."

~Luke 23:34

It's not asking to forget the wrongs that have been done or overlooking them as though they never happened or were not important. But Christ paid the price when He asked the Father to forgive. So, who am I not to forgive?

PRELUDE

I began writing my story over a period of fifteen years or more. Every time I would think about writing there was always something hindering me. I had a feeling of shame thinking how others would judge and think of me. I've since discovered that shame and fear were the two things for me not doing what God had assigned me to do.

In the last seven years, I had begun telling bits and pieces about my life. Once at our church's Women's Retreat, I spoke briefly about my molestation after being encouraged to speak up by who is now our one and only First Lady Emeritus, Ms. Ivory Shepherd. She had to nudge me because I was so fearful of speaking in front of a room filled with people, but I somehow managed to get through it.

I remember after, sitting three benches back in the middle of the row from the front, when the next young lady got up to the mic to speak and turned in my direction. With a row filled with women in front of her, she pointed her finger towards me with tears flowing down her cheeks saying,

"Because of you, because of you, I have been set free."

Well, we all began looking at one another wondering who she was really talking too when she came over and pointed her finger directly at me. I was left speechless and instantly began to cry. Those around me provided comfort and that day has always been stored in the back of my mind. Perhaps that was the pivotal point when God was showing me to try writing again or to just start sharing my testimony.

I hope He didn't give me a time limit on it because it has taken me until now to get started again. In the past couple of years, I have spoken a little about my life in front of our "Women's Ministry" gatherings. I find that I'm still somewhat nervous in front of more than two or three people. Another thing that happens is when I start telling my story people began crying, and I start crying too, so it gets hard to finish. I know at that point they're feeling sorry for me, but I really want them to know that I'm fine, because of God I've been set free.

And, the Word of God says,

"Whom the Son sets free is free indeed."

~John 8:36

Those experiences no longer have me bound. My message to my readers is that there is PROOF in the POWER of forgiveness. I no longer have to dwell on those hurtful things, and neither does anyone else, once they become set free. Not to say that some other test or trial won't come because we live in a sinful world. But when you know God and remember what He has already brought you through you can have the peace and comfort knowing that all things are working for your good in only God's timing.

We are blessed to be a blessing to others through our testimonies which is the purpose God has for my life and yours. I honestly don't know where I'd be if it had not been for God on my side. I've come to appreciate those trials and tribulations which have indeed made me a stronger person, and sensitive to the trials of others. It was only by the Grace of God and the Holy Spirit that I was awakened from the evil spirit that lulled me to sleep and kept me from realizing that somebody really loved me for me.

Soon after, I began to realize that my life's test and testimony was not for me to keep to myself, but to be able to help someone else. This is a message about a life of forgiveness and being set free. I can take no credit in this. All the glory belongs to God, our father in Heaven. I'm so grateful that he thought enough of me and trusted me to deliver his message.

I pray this book will bring you peace and comfort in whatever circumstances you may be experiencing now. Just know that God is love and He is REAL!

CHAPTER 1

My story begins with the memory of me standing in my granny's bathtub at the age of three or four with my private area exposed. I was being scrubbed down with an iodine smelling substance. My memory only allows me to see the hands washing me. Oddly enough, I cannot see the face. But amazingly after all these years I still vividly see me standing in the tub that day and I can still smell the iodine.

I didn't understand exactly what was happening at the time, but I later understood I had been molested and had developed some type of infection. The image of me standing there with everything stained orange has never escaped my thoughts.

Molestation is ugly, and it wasn't something discussed in black households during the time I experienced it. It was always a hush, hush thing especially when it came down to family members. As I grew older and came to understand more about the illness, I often wondered what kind of attraction a little girl could possess that would cause grown men to have sexual desires.

I've searched high and low for the answer and it still remains a mystery. That question has never been answered. Not by my father, my uncle, or any of the other people that were supposed to love and protect me. Instead of being protectors, some of the people I trusted most became the predators in my story.

Seriously, how is this child supposed to think, or this adolescent is supposed to act, or even now as an adult still trying to process this. Perhaps because of the money and special gifts I was given I was to think it was ok. And, up until now, this topic has never been addressed. I was the true "victim" but I felt like the bad person in the situation. I suffered from inner turmoil as my violators went on with their lives as usual.

***

During the early part of our lives, my three brothers and I lived with our fraternal grandmother. Granny as she was called, looked like an Indian squaw. After all her ancestors were of the Blackfoot or maybe the Cherokee Tribe. Not exactly sure which one, but it definitely was in her features. Granny wore two long beautiful grey braids that sometimes made a crisscrossed pattern across the back of her head. She had a beautiful light toned complexion, and she stood about 5'5" tall. Her mouth was always full of snuff, and she loved to cook while wearing a freshly starched ironed apron every single day.

21

It was something like her trademark, and it had so many colors in it that it went with whatever she was wearing.

Yes, there is a good reason why my brothers and I ended up living with our Granny. It because of something bad that happened between our parents while our Dad was still active in the military. Our brother Bernie was just a baby when daddy brought him to live with us too.

The story I was told was that my dad came home unexpectedly from military duty in Germany and found my mother in bed with another man. Coincidently this man also ended up fathering two children with my mother. My younger brothers were the King's. Well, in the midst of the struggle her lover jumped out of the window when my dad had my mother cornered. Dad sliced mom's face with a sharp knife, the cut went from her ear down to her chin. And if that wasn't enough, he also sliced her arms and legs. My mother was hospitalized for a long time.

I don't remember Dad ever going to jail for it. I believe he got off on a plea of temporary insanity and because he got away with what he did; not only did my mother hate him, but she hated us, his children ever since. It didn't matter that she had given birth to us because we reminded her of him and that was too much for her mind to handle. From that moment on, we were labeled as the Perry children and she wanted nothing to do with us.

Granny's house was home to all of us. That included her oldest daughter, my uncle who was an ex-Army man and a heavy drinker, my daddy also an ex-Army Lieutenant and drinker, Granny and us children. We all managed to live and share a comfortable two-bedroom unit, which is now called a townhouse that was located at the top of the project housing community entrance.

My baby brother and I slept in the bed with my dad, and my other brothers slept on a pallet on the floor. One thing I remember most about my Dad is that he always left money under my pillow and told me not to tell anyone.

We lived life and spent most days like all other children. We played, we ate, we were cared for, and we had fun at Granny's house until my younger brother Bernie, set the closet on fire in the bedroom where we slept. The closet was burned beyond repair and the room was filled with smoke. That very incident was the cause of the scattering and separating of the Perry children.

The Projects, where we lived with our grandmother were nice and kept up if my memory serves me correctly. Black people lived in the front of the neighborhood, and whites stayed in the back. Occasionally we would sneak back there, or they would sneak up in our area near the front to play. I don't think that anyone's family really cared because I'm sure at some point they saw us playing. Besides, we all attended the same school together. Most of my family, including aunts, and cousins lived in the same area.

We lived with Granny up until I turned nine or ten years old. My granny was nice most times although she could have a mean streak every now and then. Granny always fed us good food and there was plenty to go around. I recall seeing her wring a chicken's neck during my childhood. In a state of shock, I felt so sorry for the chicken, but that feeling vanished when it came time to eat.

Granny was particular to an extent I guess you could say because she was one to iron her pillowcases and sheets. She wasn't very strict, but she didn't play when it came to us keeping her house clean.

We were only allowed to play outdoors but if we were ever caught playing or running in her house there would be hell to pay. The front porch of the townhouse was Granny's place of refuge, it was there that she would sit in her freshly starched apron, dipping her buttercup snuff and watching everything in sight with a small switch resting on her lap.

Just call her the neighborhood hawk because she stayed on the prowl looking for mischief. If we were ever caught doing something, we had no business, we would be directed to the nearest tree and ordered to pick out our own switch. And you better not come back with something too small. Granny used her lap switch for hitting at stray cats and dogs that would wander near her flower bed after spitting out the snuff she had in her mouth for some time. Granny never needed any proof to whoop us, all someone had to do was look like they did something.

I tried not to get into trouble as best as I could because one encounter with the switch was all I needed. I was now scared for dear life. I remember like it was yesterday. I'm not sure of what I had done this time in particular, but Granny called for me to come to her. I knew I was about to get it because the tone of her voice changed when she yelled out my name. It was the first blow from the switch as I reached for the door handle. I cried and hollered for dear life and she didn't bother me again after that.

Some days after dinner my older brother Junior and I would wash dishes. We always found a way to make it fun as we hurried so we would still have time to play while it was daylight. Junior washed and I dried because

I was too short to reach in the sink. One day when I was drying the dishes as I picked up Granny's favorite big yellow glass bowl it slipped out of my hands onto the floor breaking in many pieces. It nearly gave me a heart attack. One would have thought we killed somebody. We received several licks that day as I tried to escape by crawling under the table.

The punishment I received for an honest mistake is what society today in the 21st century would refer to as "Child Abuse." There was never any reasoning that a seven-year-old who could hardly whole the bowl from the beginning could have just had an accident and nothing was done on purpose. At Granny's house back in the day there was never a need for an explanation it was just, you did it!

I don't think Granny ever considered the fact that we were little children with small hands, and the bowl was just too big and too heavy for me to handle. It's true that my Granny had her ways, but I loved her regardless because none of us were perfect.

My grandmother's youngest daughter, my Aunt Duecy as she was called lived right next door to us and the one thing, I remember frankly about her was that she loved drinking and cursing at us for no reason. At times she would hurt my brother Junior's feelings by saying her brother wasn't his dad. Alcohol turned her into a very ugly dark person at times.

Not long after an incident with my aunt being in a drunken rage, we found ourselves staying with my dad's other sisters. We were up against all types of adversity because my dad's brother never cared for us either and he waited for the perfect opportunity when our Granny was out of town to send us away. Our Dad was off somewhere in the Military oblivious of everything going on with us.

One day my brother Junior went from door to door knocking until someone finally answered. A lady by the name of Ms. Gaines who held a great resemblance to our mother. Junior looked up to her and asked, "are you my mother," with tears in her eyes, she answered no, but I know your mother and took him to where she live.

Junior came back and reported he had found Mom and felt she didn't want him there.

At the time, she had two other baby boys that were crawling around on the floor, but her change of heart came when she realized that Junior would make a good babysitter. Our Mom in her early years, passed her time hanging out at the local bars and in areas that were walking distance from her house. So, whenever she went

off on a whim, she wasn't hard to find.

CHAPTER 2

My mother back then was, and still is up until this very day, what some would like to refer to as a mystery woman. We were always told that she was from Power Tan, Virginia, but we were never able to find any record of the truth no matter how hard we searched. I remember her mentioning that she had siblings, but we had never met or seen them before. Another thing she told us was that her father was a white man and that he owned a funeral home. And just like all the other information it never came with a name, place, or a location.

One thing I do remember is visiting a nursing home with my mother one day where we saw a lady lying in a hospital bed. My brother Junior and I were told she was our grandmother, and that's the last thing I can ever recall of her. The best thing about that day I can remember is the nurse or someone gave my brother and I a bag of root beer barrel candy. It was so good and to this day I still love the taste of root beer. Whenever we asked our Mom about that side of the family, she would tell us that was her business, and for us to stay out of it. So, we did! Being young I'm sure we didn't have much of a say or choice either way.

My life was never back to normal after my mom was caught cheating by my dad. She despised us and made it blatantly clear that she didn't want us either. So, for most of our lives, we ended up living from pillar to post with this one and that one never having any stability nor a place to really call home. After a year of hopping from place to place, we eventually had to go to court or some other legal place. The person of authority seated in a leather chair behind a desk asked the four of us who did we want to live with. Myself and one of my brothers said our daddy but somehow, we all ended up staying with our mother who was not very nice to us. She only did just enough to get by, and she used every opportunity to always remind us of her hate and resentment towards our father.

Some memories of my childhood are painful when I think of them. Like that time, I walked down to the 5 & 10 store. I walked inside, picked up a bag hanging on the counter and loaded it up with goodies. I had toothpaste, toothbrushes, lotion, washcloths, combs, hair brushes, and God knows what else. But they were all things that we needed.

I didn't want to steal or become a thief, but it seemed as if I had no choice. My mother just simply didn't have a care in the world for our wellbeing. As a result of her neglect, we went through life deprived of our wants, needs, and basic necessities. Therefore, in my mind, I was just doing what I had to do. I didn't really see it as wrong.

Our mother owned a wringer washer which was kept in the cellar under the house which most of the time wasn't being used or was just broken. That meant we never had too many clean clothes or wash rags as they were called. Finding something clean looking was an adventure because you had to dig in a closet through mountains of dirty clothes or pull something out of the bathtub which was also piled with dirty clothes. A bath was out of the question. Occasionally, I would dig out a dirty slimy washcloth to try and clean myself. We wore the same dirty clothes over and over, because that was all we had.

When I walked back into my mother's house, she saw the bags in my hand.

"Where did you get all that stuff from?"

"I took it from the 5 & 10 store up the street." I said honestly. Then I got the worse beating of my lifetime.

Eventually, I stopped crying after the swelling went down and without saying a word, she walked me back to the store and made me return every item I had taken. I was so hurt that she beat me and made me return the stuff. She could have let us keep it. I was confused about that because she never bought us any of these things.

Moving on a to few years later, I remember once when I was out of grade school for the Easter holiday my mother left the house but had baked a pie and put it on top of the refrigerator. I got out of bed, pushed a chair up to the refrigerator to reach the pie where I began digging my fingers in my mother's freshly baked sweet potato pie. Hands and face all messy, I ran and jumped back in bed pulling the cover over my head as if I were sleeping. I guess I thought nobody would know that I was the one that had messed with mom's pie.

At the time I was so hungry because we hadn't eaten anything that I guess I didn't consider the consequences of what might happen. I just ate what was available. Needless to say, when my mother returned home not only did I get a whipping, but she held my hands over the fire on the stove burners because of what I had done.

Thank God my hands didn't get burned but it sure felt like it. After that terrifying ordeal, I went back and forth between my dad's sisters.

My three Aunts Mae, Mags, and Honey were the ones that took over from there. My Aunt Honey would come to get me every summer and take me to Bayonne, N.J. This is where she lived with her husband and his mother. My experiences with them weren't too bad and overall, I just wanted to be a happy kid. But then there were the times when I was being mistreated by her husband. How easy it is for a child to become confused.

At the age of 13, I was back at my mother's where I would become the babysitter for my one-year-old sister of whom I'm 13 years her senior and the one being birthed. While my mother was in the hospital having my baby sister, her live in common law husband, the father of the one-year-old, and the baby being birthed along with two other son's to later come, had come in from somewhere drinking came into where I was sleeping and tried to lay on top of me. I pushed him onto the floor and ran and got into bed with my brothers. He had a habit of always calling me pretty little thing when he was drinking. I hated that.

I don't remember him bothering me like that again although when he was drinking, he would still make those sneaky pretty little thing comments. I told my mom about what he had done and to my surprise she said, "you didn't say anything when your dad was bothering you." I never had given her remarks much thought and then one day it came to me that she knew what my father had been doing to me.

I remember the last time going back to Aunt Honey's in Bayonne, N.J. and never going back. She became where she didn't like me anymore for some reason. When I was there, she always dressed so beautifully going to work. I would still be lying in bed with Ms. Essie, her mother in law, where she would bend over to give me a kiss as she left for work. It happened whenever Aunt Honey would leave for work, that's when her husband uncle Joe would come into the room right next to his and Aunt Honey's only petitioned by a thin wall, pick me up and take me in his room lay me on his bed where he would take off my pajamas and panties. He would put his mouth on my private area and lay his penis on my vagina.

Although he never penetrated me, the experience was still traumatizing for me. I would always pretend to be sleeping while forcing my mind to go to another place. I often wonder, even now did I ever come back from where I went or if there's a part of me still floating somewhere out there in the universe. Hmmm? I recall every Friday when my Aunt would leave for work, she would never come back until Sunday afternoon. She would sit on the sofa with a blanket around her shaking and chain-smoking cigarettes with beer placed on the coffee table which she would allow me to sip the foam off the top. I liked doing that then, but today I hate the taste of beer. I thought she was cold and would put my arms around her. I never could understand why she did this every Friday. No one ever told me. Now that I'm older and wiser I believe she knew what was going on and that was her way of escape. Uncle Joe could be very mean to her and his mother sometimes and I think now maybe they were afraid of him.

I can remember staying there longer than I had normally. I even went to school from there for a brief period of time. During my tender years, my Aunt Honey and her mother-in-law Ms. Essie would love to dress me up like a baby doll, let me sit on the front steps and watch the other children across the street playing and having fun. All I could do was given an occasional wave as they waved back. I would have given up everything just to be able to play with them. I believe my caregivers where just overly protective or perhaps trying to keep the dark secret in the house. I also had two cousins that live just a couple of doors down whom I was forbidden to interact with.

It seemed like Uncle Joe, whom I stayed with, and his half-brother who happened to be married to aunt Honey's sister never interacted with one another. Even Ms. Essie, both of the brother's mother, was forbidden to visit them. That was strange, and I never found out why that was. The one sister Aunt Duecy ended up going back to Pennsylvania taking her three youngest sons and leaving the two teenage girls and boy with their father. One day while my aunt and uncle were at work, Uncle Joe's mother Ms. Essie allowed me to go over and see them. I was so excited about that, but I couldn't tell Uncle Joe or Aunt Honey. I missed my brothers back in Pennsylvania and often wondered why they could never come with me.

I did have one friend by the name of Florence, a white girl who lived right next door, that I could talk to every now and then. Our front porches connected so we could crawl across to visit one another. We got along really well and I loved her. Even though my family referred to her as "white trash," but I didn't care because she was always so nice to me. They eventually learned to overlook her family situation and allowed her to go to the corner store with me and of course Ms. Essie. She even got to go to Coney Island with me.

We were having the time of our lives when my Aunt asked the man operating the double ferris wheel to stop us on the very top. I remember holding on for dear life scared to death while Florence, laughing, kept rocking and swinging us back and forth. Believe it or not, to this day, I will not ride a ferris wheel. That incident has traumatized me for over fifty years.

CHAPTER 3

My brother's and I were now all a little older almost adolescents, and my mom allowed us to stay with her because it was beneficial. In return, she got an increase in her welfare check and monthly food stamps. I was unhappy the entire time we lived there. Most days we went hungry. Other days, Mom would send us across the street to Freeman's. The store sat directly across the street and whenever I walked in Gloria Freeman already knew what I wanted. A loaf of bread and fifty cents worth of lunch meat. The owner knew us well enough to give us credit until check day.

Once, we were outside playing in the front yard when Junior knocked on the front door to tell my mother we were hungry. We all kept saying Ma we're hungry. And we kept banging on the door because it was locked. After a while, I think we had made her upset because she opened the side window and threw the bread which fell on the ground. We still ate it because we were just that hungry. School days were unclean clothes, little to no personal hygiene, unbrushed teeth.

We almost always ate cereal for breakfast unless we were running late for school. Other than that, we had a dry government meat and cheese sandwich for lunch every day. Don't get me wrong, I always ate what I had and even liked it. Most mornings I would eat mine on the way to school because I was still so hungry from the day before.

My hunger pains were so bad that I could hardly focus when I was in school. When lunchtime came around, I would steal one of the white girl's lunches out of their locker. I know, shame on me! Because I never thought that the person I was taking from wouldn't have any lunch. The good thing that came from this was that I wasn't hungry anymore and the teacher always made up for it. when they started giving us free lunches at school, I was relieved because I knew that I would have at least one good meal.

The entire time I was in junior high school, I found myself wearing the same old brown or navy-blue skirt my mom purchased from the thrift store. I loved those skirts, but they had a noticeable hole in the back right in the center. I think most of my friends knew I didn't have much because a couple of my friends would let me borrow some of their outfits. A bath was out of the question. Most of the time as I said before, whenever you could find a washcloth in our house it would be nasty and dirty.

You had to wash the rag by hand just to take what we called a bird bath. My hair stayed dirty most of the time and my mom loved putting two uneven plats in my hair. Every morning on our way to school I would have my cousin take them out, and on the way back home, re-plat them. Of course, my mother always recognized that's not how she had fixed my hair. So, it always led to another whooping.

In my mind, I just wanted to look nice like some of my friends did. I had no idea that it was wrong to take pride in your appearance because apparently, I had gotten things mixed up and all wrong. "But God!" If it was left up to me to be the judge, I could easily determine that these conditions lead me on a stealing spree.

Over time I developed a rewarding friendship with my elderly neighbors that lived across the street from us. Ms. Stewart, and Mr. Tommy. Although as of today they're both deceased, but they live on in my memory. I made sure to wave at them whenever I saw them sitting on the porch and I also made sure I stopped by to pay them a visit. They weren't blessed to have any children in their lifetime, so they began to invest time and love into me. "But God!" That was a blessing.

Ms. Stewart took me to church with her sometimes on Sunday. My mother never took us to church. She fed me good warm meals that I learned to appreciate. Sometimes when Ms. Stewart left out of the kitchen I would sneak in the pot and steal a bite of whatever she was cooking. I made my move quick and hid behind her couch eating it so I wouldn't get in trouble. Now when I reflect back, I think she knew when I was in her pots, but she just never said anything. Ms. Stewart was aware of the living conditions over at my house, and deep down I know that's why she overlooked a lot of things when it came to me.

Ms. Stewart is the reason I was able to be Baptized at St. Phillips Methodist Church. Don't tell me God doesn't send you Angels. The baptism happened really quick. a few words were said and then someone sprinkled water on my head, and that was it. I don't know if something miraculous happened at that moment or not, but they said it did. The Pastor said that I was now born again. I wiped my forehead and took my seat back on the pew, somewhat confused at what had just happened. Later in life, my late Pastor Reverend Chauncey Smith would give me a fully emerged baptism. By that time, I had learned the real meaning of Baptism.

To my surprise, Ms. Stewart was a piano maestro. She ended up teaching me piano lessons that at first, I didn't find much interest in. She also took me to a couple of symphony orchestras that I found to be dull and boring I believe by the look on her husband Mr. Tommy's face, he felt the same way. But I didn't dare complain because anything was better than being at my mother's house. I still loved my mother regardless of how awful she treated us at times. She was still the woman that gave me life, and for that I loved her.

Mom wasn't the worst. There were times when she had a smile and a few kind words to say, especially around the first of the month when we were allowed in the living room but any other time we were locked out. When that check hit on the first the stereo blasted, everyone laughing loudly, with plenty of alcohol to drink. In a room infested with cigarette smoke.

During these times, James Brown was the hottest artist of the day. The living room speakers started vibrating as he blasted "You ain't seen nothin' yet until you see me do the James Brown."

The funny thing is that you couldn't tell my stepfather he wasn't James Brown Jr. in the flesh when he slid across the floor singing to the top of his lungs. That was the only day out of the month when friends were allowed to come over and all was a good time. Unfortunately, those moments were far and in between. Check day only came once a month, and those good times just lasted for a day. The other thirty days of the month we were absolutely miserable.

I do have a couple of vague memories of my father picking me up and taking me to get some shoes for school. They were pointed toe pixie looking shoes with multiple colors, and I loved them. I wore those shoes so much that the sole wore out on them. But that didn't matter to me. I put cardboard paper in them, so my feet wouldn't be touching the ground.

Then there was that time on my birthday when my Daddy bought me a record player, I don't really recall my age at the time, but I played my record player as much as I could and every chance that I got. I only had a couple of records, but loved to listen and sing them over and over never missing a word. While laying in my iron bed on the dirty, what used to be white, sheets. I hated that bed, because you had to lay a certain way to keep the springs from sticking you. I was the only girl at the time, so I got to sleep by myself. At that time, we lived in a three-bedroom house. Most of the time though I would run and get in bed with my brothers and lay at the bottom of the bed. There was already four of them in one bed, and of course, I made five.

They would yell at me to get out as they threatened to call mom in a low voice, but I wouldn't move even though the room reeked with the smell of stinky feet. Their worn-out shoes smelled so bad they had to put them outside their window on the rooftop. Nothing mattered. I think I was just scared of sleeping by myself and wanted to be near my brothers.

Daddy even bought me a big life-size stuffed monkey who I named Tamba. I think I also had a couple of Barbie dolls. Tamba slept in the bed with me and my dolls, so they wouldn't be cold. How silly was that? Me thinking dolls got cold. Tamba pretty much kept me in my bed as I snuggled up and laid on his chest. Tamba lasted until my mischievous brothers kept throwing him in the air and punching him. Eventually, my Tamba had to be thrown away they had knocked him around so much his stuffing was everywhere.

CHAPTER 4

Living with Mom we moved at least four times or more. 510 Summer Set St., 12 Dibert St., 210 Cherry St., and 591 Bedford St., my last residence with my mother. While residing at one of these residences, my Mom had left us home alone to go down to the local bar which was in walking distance from our house.

We were hungry, so I went into her bedroom and got the change that was laying on the dresser. I went to the corner store and bought candy for me and my brothers. I think it was only a few pennies not enough to buy food. When Mom came home and discovered that, needless to say, I again got another one of the worst whoopings. Another time she left us I went in my neighbors back yard and stole some green tomatoes. I don't know how I knew to do this, but I remember frying them on a one burner hotplate. Our gas to the stove was cut off and that was all we had. My brothers said they were good, but I don't remember. Seems like I was always in a survivor mode. "But God!"

I guess those experiences have led me to keep my promise that when I grew up, I would always have lots of food and shoes. That promise still holds true to date. Sometimes, I believe I have gone overboard especially with food and shoes. It hurts me to see someone hungry because I know very well the feeling.

Most of my ladylikeness and versatility in music is attributed to no other than Ms. Stewart. Not to mention my Aunt Honey of Bayonne, N.J. who was a fashion queen in her own way. Ms. Stewart even taught me the proper way to eat with my eating utensils, while sitting like a young lady. I love reminiscing about Ms. Stewart who always made sure I looked nice whenever she took me anywhere. I think I got separated from her when I had to go back to live with one of my aunts. Not too sure. I was moving around so much I could hardly remember one place from the next.

One day I talked my best friend into running away with me on a train. We walked down to the train station and just boarded the train. We thought everything was fine until the conductor started asking for tickets which neither of us had. We hurriedly ran into the bathroom thinking he wouldn't know we were in there, but to our surprise, he began banging on the door for us to come out. There was no escape, so we unlocked the door and slowly walked out with our heads down. The conductor made us sit down in the coach seats but not before telling us he was contacting the police and they would be waiting for us once we got to Pittsburgh which was the train's destination. I guess that wasn't a good idea at all. Once the train arrived in Pittsburgh the conductor put us out, no police in sight. We started walking towards a diner that was nearby as we pondered our next move. We knew no one there and it's starting to get dark. Both frightened to death, my best friend turns to me and said, "I'm going to call my sister and tell her to come to get us."

At that point, we had no other choice. We went to the all-night diner and waited. It was a few hours before her two sisters showed up. Both tongue lashing as we proceeded to get into the car. It was a disaster for me when I got home. Another terrible beating awaited me.

I think this episode lead me to the Cannonsburg Youth Development Center. I didn't care I just wanted to get out of my mother's house. She hated us so bad that I didn't care what happened to me. Unbeknownst to me, a couple of my Perry brothers were there also. Happened to see them at the skating field trip YDC took us on.

We later learned my mom sent us there because the judge said we were incorrigible. Which means she couldn't do anything with us. Didn't know what that word meant at the time, but since have learned about it. Mom never realized that all our acting out was the result of the mistreatment we were receiving at home by her and her common-law husband. After all, we were just kids being tossed around like a rubber ball.

My daddy came to see me a couple of times while in YDC and even brought me some nice new clothes. It was a coed campus and we were allowed to wear street clothes. The YDC wasn't all bad. Matter of fact it was better than being home. During the day we attend school on the YDC campus. The property also housed a school for the blind. That's where I met my little friend Bennie.

I would always see him on the road and say hi Bennie as they walked him to his school. After he learned my name, he would always respond back with such joy in his voice, "Hi Gloria!" Bennie was about eight years old and totally blind. Sometimes I would play a trick on him. As I came into his presence never saying a word, he would just touch me and say, "Hi Gloria." We would all get a kick out of that and wondered how he knew because I never said a word to him.

School also gave us the opportunity to smile and talk to the boys in the lunchroom. In the evening after homework dinner was served. We took turns being the clean-up crew. Floors were scrubbed and polished when necessary, and kitchen and common area spotless. Then, we were allowed to watch TV. During this time the lights were somewhat low which gave the lesbians opportunity to seek new girls and to try and cuddle inconspicuously, even though the houseparent was in eyes view.

Most of the time the houseparent had a book or was engaged in conversation with one of the other girls. Thankful for me I had a couple of straight girls who stood up for me letting them know I wasn't like that. In about a few weeks I had a so-called boyfriend. Everyone was aware of that and it was hands off. Frank was a very good-looking young man and about to be discharged in about a month. Even though there was no togetherness we always somehow made a way to communicate.

Especially at the co-ed skating parties. Passing notes at lunchtime always got the message through. Frank being discharged didn't sit very well with me. In fact, I planned and executed an escape with four of my friends I had come to trust. They called it the "Great Escape." We ran through woods and thickets that never seemed to end until we reached the city of Pittsburgh. It wasn't that far but on foot, it seemed a million miles away.

Two of the girls got caught early on, while me and the other girl named Ola who was from Pittsburgh found a place for us to stay with some of her shady family members. We moved around from place to place. Most of the people she knew were doing drugs or selling them. I was uncomfortable but had no other place to go.

After all, we were runaways and the authorities were looking for us. I really wanted to be with Frank, but that wasn't happening. He hadn't gotten out yet, so I had no way of contacting him. One day my friend Ola took me to a lady friend of her house and left me there. The lady was a drug addict. In fact, I witnessed her shooting a needle with drugs into a sore on her leg. She looked up at me and asked if I wanted some. I said no! That scared me, so I decided to leave the house and start walking.

I just started walking down what was called Hill Street, which I later learned was one of Pittsburgh's most notorious for drugs and crime. As I was walking a big car pulled up. Six men jumped out and three of them started pushing me into the back seat of the car. I tried to resist by bracing my hands on the roof of the car, but their strength overpowered me. I groaned with hope mingled with pain. "But God." This took place in broad daylight. They drove me to an isolated area in the woods where one by one they began raping me. I tried pleading and pushing them off as fear and tears ran down my face. Once they were done with me one of the guys said, "man let's just take her back." That they did and pushed me out the car back on the street almost where they had abducted me.

"But God!"

I happened to see a police car coming my way and flagged it down. I told the officers I was a runaway and had just been raped. No hospital, no nothing. I was put into the back of the police car and taken back to the YDC. I didn't get to go back to the housing area with all the other girls instead I was taken to a separate building which we called solitary confinement. No street clothes, only scrubs, and socks. Your room consisted of a bolted down iron bed, a toilet, and a sink.

The view out of the high up windows was the sky and the trees. I was locked in my room most of the time except when it came time for us to scrub the floors. Our meals were served and eaten in our room. That ordeal lasted about two weeks before I returned to my original housing area. I got to go home about a couple of months later, never serving the six months I was originally given. "But God!"

Ironically those experiences had a deep effect on me because I made a promise to myself growing up and I managed to keep it over the years. The promise was that when I grew up, I would always have food to eat and shoes for my feet. Sometimes, reflecting back on my childhood up until now I believe that there have been times when I've gone overboard but that's by no fault of my own and It always hurts when I see someone hungry because I know the feeling.

I think I returned back to my mother's house or either to my best friends. Not sure. I think I'm now about 16 going on 17, and pretty much on my own. I started hanging out with friends at local clubs that would allow us in. We even had our birth certificates changed to make sure we could get in. That's where I met this sharp-dressed, good-looking guy. He had just recently moved to our little town from Eufaula, Al. The word I got later was that he had just gotten out of prison.

He never said anything about it, and I didn't mention it either. In fact, I remember him taking me there on a Greyhound bus to go see his grandmother. It was a very long ride from Pennsylvania to Alabama. I was sort of uncomfortable or maybe even apprehensive because I had never been down south, and all I ever heard and seen on TV was how the white people hated the black. As the bus steadily moved down the road getting closer to Alabama, I kept gazing out the window seeing nothing but miles of wooded areas and what seemed like millions of trees.

The view which drove me to start thinking about the stories I heard and read about the runaway slaves. I thought to myself how incredible of a journey it must have been for slaves to be able to travel from way down here in these woods and make it up north with no shoes on their feet. I'm still amazed. Nick sat next to me and hardly said a word. It didn't matter because I was so intrigued thinking about the plight of the slaves.

Eventually, we arrived in Eufaula. Nicks cousin was at the bus station to pick us up. Alabama was very different for me. Nicks people were nice and seemed very excited to have some company. I don't think this was a place too many people wanted to visit. Nicks cousin and I went to the country store to get some pop, as we called it up north, and the store clerk acted like he didn't know what it was. Besides he didn't have the best attitude.

Eventually, Nick's cousin clarified it Nick seemed pretty nice enough so after that trip I allowed him to take me to Gary, Indiana. He got a job at the steel mill and I got a job at the White Horse Restaurant. I wondered why Gary, Indiana of all places but never bothered to ask.

CHAPTER 5

At first, everything seemed to be fine, but that relationship was not long-term because his jealousy got the best of him whereas he became verbally and physically abusive. He ended up quitting his job, going back to Pennsylvania, and I ended up moving in with my friend Laura.

One late night when we had just gotten to sleep, we were awakened by somebody yelling and banging on the door. There was a smell of smoke. The building was on fire! There was no time to get anything. Just get out! We were still in our pajamas. That's all we had. Someone drove us to a friend of Laura's. Myself, I didn't know anybody. I remember the lady there gave me a pair of dark green alligator shoes.

I loved them eventually I was able to go back to my job at the White House Restaurant. There is where I met Tommy the truck driver. He seemed like a nice enough guy so after a few dates I left Laura's and moved in with him. Tommy had a nice clean house. He was very neat and a man of few words. One day while Tommy was at work my friend, Laura came by with a couple of guys and said she was going with them to Reno, Nevada to get a good modeling job. They invited me to go.

That was right down my alley because I had always wanted to be a model. In fact, I had done a little modeling back in my home town at the local talent shows. I trusted Laura and agreed to be ready the next day. Tommy was at work, so I was leaving quietly until the guys Laura had brought with her started ransacking Tommy's house taking clothes and a gun, they found hidden in the closet. I tried to stop them and hated them for doing that because Tommy had been so nice to me.

They pushed me away. As a matter of fact, one of them became forceful. That didn't sit well with me, but my friend Laura assured me everything would be alright. Another red flag, but at my age I couldn't see it. I was always easily led. On our way to Nevada we stopped over in Chicago to pick up Tommy Walker wife Dell.

It was a long ride to Nevada. We when reached Reno the other guy was dropped off to at a hotel to wait for his girlfriend who was coming by plane. The four of us proceeded to Las Vegas. Dell had already found us a furnished two-bedroom apartment there. Laura ended up leaving me going back to Gary, Ind. because her daughter whom her husband had custody of had been hospitalized for something. I never saw her again.

Well, as the story goes Tommy Walker. and his friend were actually pimps. Tommy was very subtle about it. He was an older man beginning to grey and one who probably could have been my daddy. He had some issues going on with his back, so he had to walk slowly. I noticed that he had to lie down a lot. He drove a nice up to date Cadillac which he drove us to Vegas in. Tommy Walker wife Dell always dressed exquisitely especially when she would go out to the casinos to catch what they called a John. This was the name given for somebody soliciting sex in exchange for money.

Dell wore evening dresses, mink stoles, mink coats short and long. To see her one would think she was in show business or somebody important. Never a prostitute. She wasn't just your ordinary prostitute, in fact, their method of prostitution was using a prescription drug that she would put into someone's drink unbeknownst to them while they were at the point of being already intoxicated. Dell was very skilled at it. It didn't take long for the drug to take effect, so she had to quickly lure them to their room.

The drug made them appear as though they had too much to drink, and with her being entertained by him everybody would assume that he was drunk, and she was just helping him to his room. Her class, dress, and demeanor would keep anyone from thinking she was a prostitute or hustler. She tried to teach me this technique, but I never really got the hang of it so most of my clients got away from me. I didn't care. I knew I had to get out of this because I wasn't making any money and Tommy W was getting very upset. The only good thing about this method is that you didn't have to worry about getting undressed and having sex because by the time they got to the room they were just about knocked out.

Dell bought me nice clothes and sometimes let me wear her minks. I did this for a little while, but I never liked it I was always afraid somebody might not pass out and would hurt me. I started staying out late and began hanging with the legal age kids of one of the owners of a major Casino. They never knew I was a little poor girl from Pennsylvania. I would be out eating and drinking with them.

They never knew anything about me, and never asked. When I would come home after staying a night or two in a hotel, Tommy would get so angry with me and throw his shoe at me. He couldn't do much else because of his back problems. Dell would just look at me and never said anything. I was always so disobedient. Tommy's friend, on the other hand, had since come to Vegas and was very abusive to his girlfriend. He would beat her up if she didn't bring in a certain amount of money. Once, I saw him punch her in the face. I felt so sorry for her.

I eventually left that situation and got my own one-bedroom apartment in walking distance from the Sahara Casino. I didn't have access to the pills anymore, so I got a job at one of the casinos selling Keno tickets. By this time, I was around nineteen or twenty. I would still hang out at some of the casinos when I wasn't working. One evening I didn't have much money so was just sitting and listening to the guy planning the piano when I was approached by a nicely dressed Caucasian female.

We made casual conversation and I had a Lentz modeling brochure I had picked up laying on the table. We talked about that, and about other books she mentioned. After the music stopped, I told her I was going home. She asked me where I lived, and I told her just right across the street. Well, she insisted on driving me home and I agreed but she had to go over to the bar and get her brother. I waited and the three of us got into the car. As we proceeded to get onto the main street, I told him to turn left because that was where my apartment was.

His sister said that we're going to stop by their house for a minute to get me some books about modeling that we had talked about. They kept going in the opposite direction. I felt a fear come over me that I had never experienced. When we get to their house she and her brother jumped out. I said I would wait in the car until she came back with the books. She opened the door and insisted that I come in for a minute. I was hesitant and became even more fearful. Something down in me told me something wasn't right, but here I was. I walked into the scarcely decorated living room with just a sofa that sat low to the floor and a small TV. The brother and sister had gone into another room and I could hear someone sounding like they were talking on the phone. I sat for a moment and began calling out that I was ready to go home.

No one answered. I called out again and the man came out and said, "You're not going nowhere!" I fell to the floor on my knees and began crying. He lifted me up by my arm and escorted me into a bedroom with burglar bars on the windows. He never said anything just locked the door. The bed was made up but had a bunch of wrinkled clothes scattered all over it.

Still crying and pleading please don't hurt me, I laid on the floor with my face to the little opening on the bottom of the door and cried "Jesus help me," all night! I eventually fell asleep and was awakened by someone talking. From under the door, I could see a ray of sunlight. I began to knock really hard on the door. The women stood outside the door and told me to be quiet. I told her I had to go to the bathroom really bad. She opened the door and I ran straight towards that light which led me right outside. The man had the door open which opened to the outside and was standing there talking to a lady. Perhaps the housekeeper, I don't know.

I was running as fast as I could, hollering help me, and never looking back to see if anyone was chasing me. I got to the corner of the street and an older black man was stopped at the stop sign and said, "what's the matter baby." I pointed down the street and said they kidnapped me and took my pocketbook and stuff. He said to get in and started backing down the street. He reached under his seat and grabbed his gun. He walked up to the house where the man was still standing and said whatever you took from her go get it. The man gave him my pocketbook and we drove off. To this day, I don't remember what happened. I don't remember what the people who kidnapped me looked like, or even the face of the man that saved me.

All I know is I was saved, and shortly after that on my 19th birthday, I went back home. I had won over $10,000.00 playing craps at the Horseshoe Casino. The pit boss kept signaling me how to bet. That was the money that bought me a plane ticket back home. I had bought a wig prior to leaving and stashed all that money under my wig.

My hometown didn't have a big airport, so I landed in Pittsburgh and took cab 70 miles home. My mother wasn't excited about seeing me, but she was ok when I gave her some money and bought her a new living room suite. I gave my brothers some money too. The next day, I went to the car dealership and bought myself a backdrop top navy-blue Cadillac which resembled the Batmobile, and we'd ride all around town.

My girlfriends and I would go down to the local teen spot where we gathered to dance, eat hamburgers and just hang out. That's where I met this guy who I really didn't like but somehow ended up living together with him. He was nine years older than me. He was one that you would call tall dark and handsome. Had a processed hairdo and wore nice shoes and clothes. You could say he was attractive.

He had a place that was above and behind his mother's house and "speak easy" that she and her common-law husband ran. His mother and her common-law husband treated me very nice. I had a problem with her common-law husband because he began offering me money for sex. He would come around when D and his mother weren't home, and say you know this is my house and I let you stay here for free. I refused but he would say he only wanted to touch me. I let him because I needed the money.

This would happen about once a month. I felt so dirty. I was glad he was old and really couldn't do anything else. I took the money and began fixing the place up real nice. D wasn't a very tidy person, so I had a lot to do to get the place livable when I first got there. I eventually got a little part-time job down at the walking distance grocery store, so I was able to help out with fixing the house and buying the groceries.

D had a job painting. The relationship started off ok, but every time D would start drinking, he would get drunk and started getting violent. On one occasion I made him some spaghetti and I don't remember what was wrong with it, but he took and threw it out in the backyard and came back and knocked me over the oven door which was open at the time. He started missing days of work and going off and staying for days at a time and expected me to still be there when he got back. The talk was that he was dating a girl by the name of T in the small town of Altoona which was about maybe two hours away.

He even fathered two of her children while we were together. Sometimes I would go to Altoona with him to a club or someone's party. He would get drunk, fall asleep and I had better be sitting right there when he woke up or I would be beaten. Once he took me to a club in our area and we sat at the bar, his preference. We sat there facing the front door.

I sat with my head down. Then the door opened I happened to look up. He backed handed me and I fell to the floor. His remark was what you looking at that nigger for? This type of abuse went on for several years. I didn't have the courage to leave because I had become so fearful of him and felt I had nowhere to go, he always threatened to kill me. Most of the people he hung around with were afraid of him to so when he was beating me, they did nothing.

One wee hour in the morning D and his cousin came in after being gone for a couple of days, reeking of alcohol and cigarettes I pretended to be asleep. His cousin laid on the couch in the living room and he came and got in the bed. I waited until he got good and asleep then got out of the bed, got some pantyhose and tied his hands to his neck, then his hands to his feet. I made sure he couldn't get loose. I got some matches out of his pocket, pulled the sheet back and began trying to set the mattress on fire. It wouldn't seem to catch on fire, just started smoldering. I ended up putting it out because I didn't really want to do that besides his mother lived downstairs.

So, what I did do was tie his hands and feet to the pantyhose I had around his neck. so, he couldn't move without choking. I then started sticking him with a pencil until he woke up. He finally did and started struggling to get out of those pantyhose and cursing me saying he was going to kill me when he got out. Meanwhile, his cousin who had been out all night with him was in the living room laughing. Never coming to his aide.

When I saw he might be getting loose I ran out the house up the hill to one of my friend's house, I stayed there most of the day and then called his mother to see if he was there. She said no, and I came back and stayed down in the "speak easy" with her. One of the regular neighbors was sitting there, drinking beer with her. D eventually came home and stopped down first at the "speak easy." A place black folks gathered to purchase illegal beverages. It was run by his mother and her common-law husband.

This was always his first stop. I was sitting there beside his mother and he laughed and said, "you got me this time!" He never got me back for that. I think that was the beginning of me coming out of my fear. D's sister offered me to come and stay with her because she knew how abusive he was. His sister's husband who is an army officer, threatened him if he ever came near his house to bother me.

That worked as long as he was home, but it didn't totally stop him because after all, that was D's sister. I didn't want to cause problems for D's sister and her family, so I decided that wasn't the best place to be because he would come around and start cursing in the presence of her children.

CHAPTER 6

In the meantime, I had started dating a cousin on his sister's husbands' side, who had recently come home on leave from the Coast Guard. We ended up having a one-night stand and I became pregnant. I stayed with his sister until after my son was born. One day her brother came to the house when his sister and her husband were gone.

One of his young nieces had let him in. I was upstairs taking a nap with my baby on my chest when he came up in the room and hauled off and slapped me in the face. His nieces told their mother and father what he had done, and his sister said to me because of the way her brother acts she doesn't want this going on around her children. So, she asked me to leave. I understood so

I took my baby and we went down the street to my cousin Gloria's and her husband J. They had never had any children and were happy for us to be there. I later asked my cousin could my good friend Eve come and stay with us because she had recently divorced and found herself outdoors.

They agreed. Once again, I'm being approached in a sexual way by my cousin's husband. It seems like everywhere I went somebody was making sexual advances at me. I couldn't say anything to her about it because I was afraid that she would put me and my baby out and I didn't know where else I could take him and be safe. I ended up staying with my cousin Gloria and her husband about a year. Being there with her gave me an opportunity to enjoy life a little because she loved keeping my son. Later on, I married my son's father who now was out of the military. We ended up getting a nice house and I became pregnant with my second son. I brought my best friend Eve to live with us. She had also lived with me at my cousin Gloria's.

My house became sort of a hangout place on the weekends. We lived in walking distance of the downtown area. When friends or relatives would buy a new album or record, they would always stop by and wanted us to hear it. Most of the time, they ended up staying all day smoking marijuana and having something to eat. As soon as others saw friends' cars at the house, they joined in.

Everybody was always peaceful and respectful. Back in those days, marijuana was the thing to do. You get high, sit there, nod, and get the munchies. Someone always brought sweets to satisfy the munchies. I never cared much for it because it made me feel like I wasn't in control.

My husband and I both worked in the coal mines. That was not my job of choice, but my brother Randy had just returned home from the Marines and was looking for a job. At that time Bethlehem Coal Mines were hiring. They paid a very good salary. I took my brother to the job site, where all the men were filling out applications. I sat there for a while and decided I would fill one out too just to be doing something, I really wasn't looking for a job in the coal mine, just didn't want to sit idle.

Well, as the story goes when I presented my application to the interviewer, he Immediately said "We're not hiring women." I then pointed out to him on the application where it said no discrimination between sex, creed, or color. His exact words were, "you got a point there." A couple of weeks passed, and I thought no more about it until I received a "you're hired" letter in the mail, I couldn't believe they called me and not my brother.

Thinking back though, I believe it was the bottom line I showed the interviewer on the application. Now, since they called me it was time for me to show up. The first day we were given safety information and other valuable information that required the job to get down. To my surprise, there were two other women that had been hired the same time. One Caucasian, and the other Hispanic.

We received our helmet, goggles, a large belt which held our 31b battery pack that supplied energy to the light we had on our helmet. That was one of the most necessary items we had to have. If your light went out, it was a darkness that you could never imagine. It was like being buried alive. Occasionally, we would have to turn our lights off to go to a somewhat deserted area to use the bathroom, there weren't any toilets down there. You stayed there your whole shift unless you got sick. We were told we had to wear steel-toed boots. Our lunch had to be brought in a metal container. The purpose of that was to keep the mice/rats from eating it. Believe it or not those rodents were purposely put in the coal mine as a safety precaution in case of a cave in. Whichever way they ran we were to run in the same direction.

Their keen senses knew where to find an opening or fresh air. I only worked there for one year. We rode an elevator shaft 800 ft down, drove about three miles in by way of what looked like a flat low to the ground military vehicle. It was all metal to help withstand any fallen debris. Sometimes the areas that we had to go in you had to bend down, or even crawl. My job was to drive what was called a buggy car. This vehicle followed behind what was called a miner that dug the coal out and placed it onto my vehicle.

Once filled, I backed away and drove a short distance to a conveyor belt and emptied the coal. The conveyor belt took the coal to the outside where it emptied into a boxcar to be taken for processing. Sometimes, I had to lift 50 lbs. bags of rock dust and spread it around the mined area to keep the coal dust down.

At other times I helped build, what was called brandishes or small brick walls. The purpose was to keep the air in the mine flowing a certain way. Sometimes that area was pretty cold. We also had to put up large tarps for the same purpose. I always tried to look prissy with makeup and perfume prior to going in the mine. But coming out you couldn't tell me from one of the guys.

CHAPTER 7

My first son Sean was two at the time and I had had another son Ray who was named after my husband. We did pretty well for a while, but my husband made a lifestyle of drinking and doing drugs. He was ok when he wasn't drinking but then he started becoming violent. He started staying out and even fathered another child while we were married. I told him I wanted him to get out, but he wouldn't so I went to get my cousin who nobody messed with and he stayed there until I got my things out and left.

I took my children and went back to cousin Gloria's. It was starting to get cold, so we stayed throughout the winter then I started looking for an apartment. Gloria didn't want us to leave, but she was getting too attached to my children as if they were hers. I found a house on the other side of town and my friend Eve moved in with us. She was good keeping the boys while I worked at Metropolitan Ins. Co. I would take the boys sometimes over to their grandparents who lived about 45 minutes away.

One day while I was home alone the landlord came over and asked me was everything ok in the house, I told him it was. He came towards me and tried to kiss me. I pushed him away and he said, "you know you want me." I told him to get out. He did leave, but it wasn't long after that I move into the newly built projects. The area was nice and clean and there was a mixture of people there. Even some of my relatives lived there. I hooked up with another friend who was from D.C. and we became inseparable. When you saw her, you saw me. My friend Eve had gotten hooked on drugs and had moved on again. I never saw her again after that last time. I heard a few years ago that she had passed away. The talk was the drugs had brought her down. My D.C., friend and I wore the same size clothes and shoes.

I could go to her house whenever I wanted and borrow something to wear. She didn't even have to be home. She could come to my house and do the same. We were just that close. We would hang out on the weekend at the Elks Club or one of the other two clubs. Always dressed to the T. We were at a private party on a Friday night and there I met my second husband who had just moved to our hometown from Buffalo, N.Y. He was really nice, and so was his family. We started dating for a little while and I became pregnant with our daughter Tia. This relationship lasted a few years until I discovered or perhaps in my insecurities thought he was cheating with the girl he was giving a ride to work. Well, after that I couldn't trust him and asked him to leave. He left and went to stay with his cousin. Meanwhile, my husband's brother and his wife had relocated to the Atlanta area and were telling him how great it was there. My husband and I ended up getting back together.

So, we ended up packing and moving there to Decatur. We piled in with my brother in law for a couple of days until our apartment was ready which we had already put in for prior to moving there. I enrolled the boys in school and found a babysitter in the building next to mine. My husband got a job in construction, and I ended up being the apartment manager. That worked out really well because we didn't have to pay rent. I did that for a couple of years until the property owner sold the property and they brought in their own managers. The marriage somehow didn't work out, and we got a divorce. My husband immediately started dating another woman whom he married and ended up with a daughter a year or two younger than ours, and I started dating someone else too. About a year later, my boyfriend and I moved in together. Things were going pretty well I thought.

We bought a nice house and had a couple of nice cars. He was a long-haul truck driver. Who had relocated to Georgia from Alabama. He said I didn't have to work, and I didn't. I just was the Leave It to Beaver mother. Took the kids to school, picked them up, made sure there were snacks in the basket and had dinner ready every evening at six. We eventually sold that house and moved to Griffin, Ga on nine acres of land with a spring stocked fishing lake, and a screened in porch over-looking the lake. We had a lot of work to do getting that place livable the way we wanted it. After a lot of money, sweat, and tears we had it just the way we wanted it. Prior to us owning it an older white lady had it and when she died her grandsons lived in it. They kept the place like a pig pen. Had motorcycles all in the living room.

My boys were teenagers now and had become rebellious, and hard-headed. I kept getting warned that if I didn't do something about them, we would all be put out. The saddest day of my life came when we had to take my boys to Pennsylvania to live with their father and his wife. I thought they would be ok there. I didn't know their dad and his wife had become Jehovah Witness and were forcing their religion on the children. As time went on, they began staying with someone else. Their dad and his wife eventually separated. The boys were living pillar to post as I learned later. The boys later ended up moving to Harrisburg, Pennsylvania with their dad's niece. Without proper supervision, they ended up getting into the drug life.

They always liked dressing nice and fast money seemed to be the answer. It wasn't a good idea apparently, because Sean, the oldest ended up going to prison for a couple of years. I went to visit him and told him when he got out, he needed to go into the Military. I had been telling them that, but they always said they didn't want a white man telling them what to do. Most of their life we didn't communicate because, they told me later, they didn't want me to be connected to their lifestyle.

I learned later the youngest son had become a pretty big time in the business. He had even served time in the penitentiary for drug dealing. He had used some of the money to purchase a laundromat and a convenience store, which he eventually lost. During his drug season, he ended up with a girlfriend and a couple of kids and moved back to Georgia not far from me but only stayed a short period of time.

Their friends and contacts were in Harrisburg and that's where they wanted to be. Ray got out of the drug dealing and got a legal job as assistant night manager for the Marriot where he stayed. I understood from his brother that he was always a marked man because he wouldn't give up the "Big Boys."

His girlfriend and he had gone their separate ways and he was with somebody else. My son and my relationship picked back up and he would call me at least two or three times a week.

CHAPTER 8

One Friday afternoon the weekend of Memorial Day, he called me all excited that the manager of the Marriot offered him to be the overall night manager because he had such good work ethics and would work many long hours. I was excited for him and told him that was a blessing. Ray was on his way to pick up his brother Sean to come with him to his girlfriend's son's basketball game.

On the way, Ray received a phone call from a guy who Ray had helped by putting money on his books when he was in prison. The guy told Ray he had some money to give him for helping him out and to meet him at a certain restaurant. The guy gets in the SUV as I was told they talked for a few minutes and the guy goes his way. Ray and Sean are on their way to the basketball game and get pulled over by the police.

They were made to get out the vehicle and it was searched with dogs for drugs. My sons sat on the ground while this was going on. They didn't find anything but confiscated his wallet, and the $100 bill he had laying on the console. They went on about their weekend and the day after Memorial Day the police called Ray to come down and get his wallet. Well, he said he didn't feel good about it but went anyway.

That was the last time he was a free man. I got a call from his girlfriend around 10:10am explaining to me what happened. I got to talk to my son, and he said mom they have me for dealing drugs to the guy I met with. He said I sold drugs before big time, but I didn't do this. The police framed me with this guy. His girlfriend and I immediately started getting the money together trying to get him a good lawyer, I got in thousands of dollars of debt trying to help my son not to go to prison.

His employer and other co-workers tried to speak on his behalf, but the judge wasn't hearing it. They even brought in his brother in who they threatened with jail time if he didn't testify against him. We've been up to see him several times. We write and send money. We're still trying to retain another lawyer. To date, he still in jail. The blessing is they sent him to a minimum-security federal institution. This is enough to make a person lose their mind.

"But God!"

I am remarried now. Everybody has grown up, and we have grand and great-grandchildren. There's still so much to tell, but it would take a lifetime and I'm at a point in my life that all I strive for is love and peace, continuing to pray for Mercy for my children and grandchildren who some of them have started out on the wrong track. Satan couldn't destroy me, so he went for my children. But I'm reminded of the Word of God that says,

"The Lord will perfect those things that concern me."

~ Psalms 138:8.

I don't worry about anything because God keeps me in perfect peace, and I take Him at His Word. He's a God of timing, and I may not see the things I'm praying for in my lifetime, but I know he's able. In summary, over a period of over twenty plus years, I suffered under the hand of evil men and some women, just trying to find somebody to love me. My body being abused, battered, beaten, treated like dirt, kidnapped, taken advantage of, misunderstood, my mind confused. All I can say is, "But God!"

Experienced multiple bad relationships and marriages still trying to find love.

"But God!"

As time went on, I found myself going back to Pennsylvania on several occasions to see my mother, dad, and other siblings that were still living there. My brother Randy had gone on to make his home in Houston, Texas where "The Shoe Shine Boy", as he was called, ended up doing very well. So, deserving he was always so giving to others. Several of our other siblings found their way to Houston also. Myself, and my sister Carol whom I brought to Georgia after she graduated still remain here. I wish our relationship was better though.

One day I received a call from my brother Bernie who was still living in Johnstown close to daddy. He told me that my dad was in the hospital and he wasn't doing very well. I immediately got my things together and caught a flight to Pittsburgh the nearest major airport to my city. I rented a car and drove straight to Memorial Hospital.

A few years ago, dad, had his left leg amputated. He was still able to live somewhat of a normal life. He was even able to drive his car. Daddy still drank alcohol and smoked cigarettes more than he should have and didn't take the best care of himself. Somehow the amputated area got infected and here he was. I loved my dad, always kept in touch with him and we never discussed what he had done to me. As I entered the room, there wasn't this 6ft tall man with the pretty black mixed with grey hair looking at me, but a frail shrunken body covered with a white sheet up to his neck. Daddy looked over at me as I was entering the room and managed a smile while saying in a weak voice. "Gloria I'm Sick."

Leaning over with tears in my eyes to kiss his forehead, I said, "I know daddy Bernie told me that's why I'm here." Something came over me and with tears streaming down my cheeks I told my daddy to repeat after me and I began saying the Lord's Prayer. I really don't know if I was saying it right, but my dad with his weak voice and tears flowing down his cheeks began repeating after me.

I believe till this day in my heart of hearts that my Dad went to Heaven because I believed God honored our prayer. That prayer was saying daddy I forgive you, and for him asking for forgiveness. Look at God! He can turn what was so wrong into something so right. I stayed a little while longer, kissed him and left the room. Never to see him alive again.

I went to visit my mother, aunties, cousins, and a few friends while I was home and left for Georgia the next day. It was just a couple of days later when I received another phone call from my brother Bernie saying my dad had just died. I cried so hard over the phone. I was so glad I went to see my dad and said the "Lord's Prayer" with him.

I didn't want my dad to go to hell for what he had done to me. Saying this, I was just a casual churchgoer when I went to see my daddy. As I have grown spiritually, I know that it wasn't anyone but the "Holy Spirit" that had been leading and guiding me. "But God!"

On one occasion, I tried to contact my aunt and uncle whom I stayed within New Jersey. But when I called my Uncle Joe said Aunt Honey didn't want to talk to me. I never understood that. She was one of the ones that took care of me. I never spoke to my aunt nor my uncle again. I heard she had become sick and one of her older nieces brought her back to Johnstown to take care of her. She had ended up losing her mind and eventually passing away. All of my aunts and uncles on my dad's side have passed away. To date, we still have never met anyone from my mother's family.

CHAPTER 9

After finding myself, I did end up going back and getting an education in Business Administration. I also, went to Howard University. for a brief period while living in D.C., I didn't graduate though. I got a job and went back home to my aunts for a while. In Georgia besides being an Apartment Manager, I managed what was called the "Passport Restaurant and Bar" at Hartsfield Int'l Airport. I left there after the new owner fired the present help.

Then I later got a job with a trucking company in the payroll office. Worked there several years until accepting a buy- out. That was a good choice on my part because the company eventually ended up folding. And after that, I got a job with an eye center while picking up my daughter's glasses. I wasn't really even looking for a job, but I remember riding down the highway on 75 S and saying to myself admiring that building I would like to work there and here I was, dressed in jeans not even presentable for applying for a job. Making small talk as I waited for my daughter to be fitted for her glasses. I asked one of the front desk receptionists if they were hiring.

She immediately said yes and beckoned for the office manager who said I needed to fill out an application. Well, I just ended up talking to the office manager and several other front desk personnel who kept searching for an application. None could be found. After several minutes of conversation, I left my phone number with the office manager, she said would give me a call next week.

I got a call that Monday asking when I could come to work. I told her in about a week once I got everything situated. At that time my husband really didn't want me to work, but things weren't going so well, and I knew eventually I would need a job. While working at that job, one of the Eye Doctors was offered an eye center by a Doctor's wife who wanted to get rid of it since her husband had recently passed away with a massive heart attack. As a matter of fact, he was a friend of the deceased. I was asked to be his manager. There I stayed until I took early retirement.

The Lord blessed me with my present husband, Cornell Stevens which brings me to how we got together. I met Cornell on my birthday after reluctantly telling my friend Nita I didn't want to go anywhere for my birthday. It was on a Friday evening, I had just come in from work. My weekend was all planned. The phone rings and my girlfriend asked what are you doing for your birthday? My reply was, "I'm going to lay on my couch, eat, and watch the Lifetime Movie Marathon." She replied, "Girl it's your birthday you need to do more than that."

We went back about me not wanting to out. Finally, she said just let me take you out to dinner. She came over and started looking in my closet for something I could put on. Prior to her coming I had said I had nothing to wear. It was getting to be around nine o'clock and I said it's too late to go eat I don't eat this late. Her next words were, "we could just go to the Talisman?"

I turned and said that's where you wanted to go anyway. She went on to remind me that today was her daughter's birthday too, and she would be their checking ID at the door. Besides, she said the owner had prepared a lot of food. The Talisman was a local club and always a great place to eat, the food was delicious, we frequented that place a lot and were friends with the owners. Needless to say, we ended up at the Talisman sitting at the bar which was Nita's favorite place to sit. Me, I like sitting down in the table area by the dance floor.

My friend Nita had gotten engaged in conversation with **a** gentleman visiting from the Washington D.C. area who just happened to be sitting on the left side of her and she had forgotten all about me. I ordered a glass of wine and just sat there looking bored with my elbows on the bar and my face cuffed in my hands. The bartender came by occasionally and checked to see if I needed anything.

Not much was happening on my end of the bar, but sometime after midnight the door next to me opened and in walked this tall, dark, nicely dressed, with shine shoe man. I nudged my friend and said, "Nita there's somebody for you." She was tall, and I thought that

113

might be a good fit. She slightly turned to look and kept talking to the guy next to her. The man that came in proceeded to walk towards the dance floor area and the small bar where you ordered food to-go. Still bored, I decided I would go to the lady's room.

Back to my seat, still bored. The guy that I was trying to show her started walking back our way and I said, "Nita, here he comes again." She didn't look this time, and he walked passed me to the patio door. A few minutes later Nita's daughter came in with the photographer to show us the picture he had just taken of her. As I commented on how nice it was he told me my friends daughter had let him know it was my birthday also and he wanted to take my picture too.

I stood up to stand against the wall that was behind me, and he said, "no, no I have a backdrop outside." I proceeded to follow him outside and behold the gentlemen I was trying to show my friend was sitting at the outside bar.

As I walked up, he padded the seat next to him saying, "If you need a seat, here's one right here." I smiled and said no thank you, I'm just getting my picture taken. Then he said, "take two or three of them I'll pay for them, but you have to give me one."

I couldn't help but give him a picture. He had made me laugh. We sat and talked for the rest of the evening. We went inside and danced a couple of times. Especially to Tevin Campbell's song, "Can we talk for a minute." Seems like that was right on time.

My friend went over to get her. Nita said she was hungry and wanted to go to the Waffle House just down the street. The guys decided they would go too. My friend that I was talking to said I could ride with him, Nita said, "she doesn't know you." He replied, "I'm a perfect gentleman." He proceeded to open the door of his Chevy Blazer for me. We ate and talked at the Waffle House until it was almost daylight, when we all decided to part. My friend said don't forget to call me. He had told me his number earlier and I had memorized it. I didn't answer, just got into Nita's car.

Well, I let a whole day go by before I called him. When I did decide to call him and said hello, when he answered the phone there was so much excitement in his voice by the way he said "HI." His next words were, "thought you were going to call me yesterday." I quickly responded by saying, "I'm calling you now." We laughed and talked the whole day until it was time for him to leave work. He had it like that at work. At the end of the conversation, he asked for my number.

I told him I couldn't give it to him because I was currently in a relationship that was about to end, and I wanted to do things right by waiting until my friend got back from out of town. He promised me if I gave him the number he wouldn't call until I said it was ok. I believed him, and we hung up. Moments later my phone rings, who was on the other line the one that said he wasn't going to Call me, saying, "HI." I immediately said, "I thought I told you not to call me."

His response was that he was checking to see if I had given him the right number. Of course, that quick thinking brought a laugh out of me, I couldn't be mad.

CHAPTER 10

Once my friend who was actually serving 30 days for a 3rd DUI was released from jail I broke up with him. I let my new friend know that I was free. He told me he was recently divorced and free too. We dated for a year, and just as he prophesied that night when I met him on my birthday I would be his wife, that day came true.

We met on what I thought was my birthday May 6th, but it was actually May 7th because he didn't come in the place until after work which was after midnight. Look how God was working in that. We got a reasonable package to Vegas for $580.00 Which included a two-night stay at the Casino Hotel, a Limo ride to the courthouse for a license, and service at the chapel.

This is May 6th my wedding day. We've gotten dressed in our wedding attire all prepared for the limo to take us to the courthouse. Outside the courthouse were lots of people dressed in various outfits, some kind of weird, but that's Vegas. All were waiting to get their license. Of all days, the courthouse was closed. Nothing is supposed to be closed in Vegas. What a big disappointment. The next day May 7th we started out again. With our marriage license in hand heading to Graceland Chapel. Better known as Elvis Presley Chapel. There we exchanged vows. My husband looked at me in a way I will never forget. The sincerity in what he said, and that look will always be engraved in my heart. We were married, just he and I, the preacher and the witness.

As we became closer to the Lord and quit the clubbing scene, we could see the Lord's hand in our relationship. My husband and I had frequented this same club on a regular basis, yet our paths had never crossed. We both knew the owners and all the other personnel that worked there. Looking back, we could now see when it was time for our paths to cross and for us to become one, it was orchestrated by God. He wouldn't allow us to get married until the 7th which is the number of "Completion."

My husband Cornell and I are now members of the Greater Travelers Rest "House of Hope Atlanta." Serving under the most awesome, humble, anointed Pastor/Teacher this side of Heaven. None other than the one and only Dr. E. Dewey Smith, Jr. His teaching and preaching abilities have been such a tremendous blessing in the spiritual growth of our lives. We are so very grateful for serving under his leadership.

Currently, my husband serves as a Deacon, and I, a Deaconess. We both serve in various other ministries at the "House of Hope Atlanta."

Lastly, but not least. I want to thank God for giving me another mother. She's never had children she's given birth to, but I call her my mother because she has shown me the love and kindness of a mother I never had. We always enjoy doing things together and spending countless hours on the phone. I'm welcomed as part of her family. I love her dearly and thank God for her. She is no other than, Mother Mary Houston Kennedy.

God always knows who to put in your path in your time of need. Just trust Him. He knows what's best for us. Every day God has been helping me, giving me protection, comfort, and wisdom. Real help that I cannot deny. Nothing is more valuable than learning and knowing from experience that God is trustworthy, and God is REAL! Thank you, God!

And finally,

"But may the God of all grace, who called us to His eternal glory by Christ Jesus, after you have suffered a while, perfect, establish, strengthen, and settle you. To Him be the glory and the dominion forever, and ever."

~1Peter 5:10

Gloria Perry Stevens Biography

Gloria Stevens is a fun loving, hospitable, and compassionate first-time author who resides in Georgia with her husband of whom she says she has created a "bowling maniac." She also enjoys the game herself. Especially when it comes to traveling to participate in tournaments all over the country. She writes her story of forgiveness from her own life experiences hoping to ignite in others that may find it hard to forgive to experience the healing, peace, comfort, and most of all being released from the bondage of not being able to forgive. She believes we must allow ourselves to put aside our feelings and emotions and in turn be guided by the love, compassion, and mercy that has been given to us.

Made in the USA
Columbia, SC
04 February 2020